The Complete
Book
of
Wedding Toasts

WEDDING TOASTS

The Complete
Book
of
Wedding Toasts

JOHN WILLIAM MCCLUSKEY

ARDEN BOOK COMPANY
EAST HAMPTON, NEW YORK

Published by
Arden Book Company
P.O. Box 4084
East Hampton, New York 11937

The Complete Book of Wedding Toasts
First Edition
ISBN 0-9677332-0-0

Book design by Lois Frevert

Manufactured in the United States of America
Published simultaneously in Canada

Acknowledgments

The author wishes to express his thanks to the following publishers for their kind permission to reprint poems copyrighted or controlled by them:

"Married Love," by Kuan Tao-Sheng, translated by Kenneth Rexroth and Ling Chung, ©1972 by Kenneth Rexroth and Ling Chung. Reprinted from *The Orchid Boat: Women Poets of China* by permission of New Directions Publishing Co., New York.

"First Love," by John Clare, reprinted with permission of Curtis Brown Ltd, London, on behalf of EricRobinson. Copyright Eric Robinson 1984.

The poems contained in our Great Poets and Sages section were taken from:

Masterpieces of Religious Verse, edited by James Dalton Morrison, ©1948 by Harper & Brothers Publishers, New York and London:
   "True Love," by James Russell Lowell; "Love," Author Unknown; "Marriage," by Wilfred Wilson Gibson; "O God of Love, To Thee We Bow," by William Vaughan Jenkins; "What God Hath Promised," by Annie Johnson Flint.

Poems That Live Forever, Selected by Hazel Felleman,

To my wife, Lois, who after more than three decades, leaves me feeling happy enough about marriage to write this book.

To our children: Carolyn, Sharon, Brian, Diana, and John, all of whom have brought us happiness beyond our wildest hopes.

WEDDING TOASTS

Table of Contents

Introduction

The main purpose of this book is to give inspiration and confidence to people who are anxious and, yes, fearful of making a toast or giving a speech. If you are one of these individuals, don't feel you are alone—far from it. A well known survey identified fear of public speaking as the number one fear of most people queried—even ahead of death!

There are several things one can do to overcome nervousness. For one thing, most wedding dates are announced many months, and sometimes years, in advance. The key to your success lies in the preparation of your toast and then practice, practice, practice. If you postpone preparation until the day before, you should not be surprised to find that you are a touch anxious about the outcome.

First, read through this book. You are certain to find an appropriate toast for the occasion. Use a toast that works well with the ideas you've formulated on your own. You may want to take a line from here and one from there while composing your own personal salute. Or you could combine two or three of our toasts, or quote from one of the beautiful poems we've included in our "Great Poets and Sages" chapter. Make it personal, deliver it from the heart and you can't go wrong!

Author's Note

The idea for this book was started over 30 years ago. In fact, in 1970 I wrote the introduction and a few dozen toasts. The file kept building up over the years, taking inspiration from various sources from all over the world. Slowly the file grew until I decided to organize the notes I had made on bits of napkins, scraps of paper, and on tape recordings, into the book that you see here.

All the toasts were edited by my wife, Lois. In addition to these original toasts, there is a chapter on Great Poets and Sages, as well as selections from the Old and New Testaments. The verses quoted came from the Revised Standard Version and the New American Bible, both published by Thomas Nelson Publishers.

I hope you enjoy using this book. My hope is that it will give you the material to make a meaningful, personal tribute—one that will be remembered long after the wedding is over.

John McCluskey
Amagansett, NY
December 1999

The Complete
Book
of
Wedding Toasts

WEDDING TOASTS

The Tradition

Toasting has an ancient history among civilized people—Vikings, Chinese and Romans all toasted each other's health and good fortune. It was understood that the host would always be the first one to drink from the cup to prove that the drink was not poisoned.

The Vikings are credited with the first regular usage of the toast. It was their custom to welcome visitors in from the cold with a bowl of warm beer, kept in a vessel called a skoal. The toast, "skoal," is still in common usage in Scandinavian countries and throughout the world.

Today, a wedding combines two very old traditions—the toast and the speech. This book is mainly devoted to the toast, that poetic combination of words that beautifully bespeaks the joy of the moment and the event. By combining several of our quotes and adding some pertinent, personal information about the bridal couple, you will be able to deliver a memorable, concise tribute.

Toasting has become an integral part of the wedding, and, indeed, all the traditional social events leading up to the wedding and reception. The events where toasting is expected are many. Here are some of them:

THE ENGAGEMENT PARTY

Traditionally, the father of the bride, stepfather, grandfather, or any special male friend, may make the first toast. It is also appropriate for the bride's mother to make the first toast, particularly if she is the one hosting the party. Then the groom toasts the bride and her family. And then, of course, anyone who wishes may toast to the happiness of the couple.

THE BRIDAL SHOWER

The shower begins the cycle of wedding celebrations and is often attended these days by men as well as women. The shower offers lots of opportunities to toast and make speeches. The maid of honor, the bridesmaids, and the host of the event, should all toast the bride to be.

THE BACHELOR PARTY

The bachelor party has a long-standing tradition of toasting and speechmaking by the male members of the wedding party and friends of the groom. It is also appropriate for the groom to toast his bride-to-be, her family, and members of the wedding party.

THE BRIDESMAIDS' LUNCHEON OR BACHELORETTE PARTY

The traditional luncheon and/or night on the town provide many opportunities for toasting and speeches. The bridesmaids toast the bride, the mother of the bride toasts her daughter, and the bride toasts everyone—her mom, the wedding party and, of course, the groom.

THE REHEARSAL DINNER

This dinner is usually hosted by the parents of the groom for the entire wedding party, the immediate family and close friends. The mother and father of the groom begin the toasts to the happy couple and the bride's family. The best man toasts the couple, the groom toasts the bride and her family, the bride toasts the groom and his family. This is the traditional time for the bride and groom to give gifts to the wedding party in thanks for their participation in the wedding. Emotions usually run high at this event and many toasts are the norm.

THE WEDDING RECEPTION

The Main Event. As one of his most important duties, the best man delivers the first toast of the celebration. He can include how the couple met, some history of their relationship, and conclude with a wish for their future together. This is the first, and one of the most important, toasts of the day. If done well, it can actually set the tone for the rest of the party.

The groom may thank the best man for his good wishes and then toast his new bride and her family. The bride can then toast her groom and his family. Other toasts usually follow by other friends and family members.

After the wedding, celebrations can continue throughout the next day, at breakfasts, brunches, and luncheons. Here again, let us toast the bride and groom!

Helpful Hints

A s in most things, preparation is the key. You will probably want to customize your toast to the bride and groom. If you are not sure of some of the pertinent events leading up to the nuptials, ask the bride and groom for the facts. They will be more than happy to share the information with you. And remember, there is no such thing as a dumb question.

Keep your toast or speech short and simple— brevity is not considered a character defect! Remember, for most people the rate of speech while speaking in public is 150 words per minute. Decide beforehand how much time is appropriate for the occasion, and what you can objectively deliver without difficulty. Remember, there really are no rules regarding time, except one: don't overburden yourself or the audience. Better you err on brevity's side than you ramble on too long.

Use simple words and phrases—you will be far less liable to fumble or get tongue tied. Practice in front of friends or family members. Visiting the site of the reception is very helpful in making you feel more comfortable about your surroundings.

If you choose to use quotes in your toast, don't say, "quote, unquote." Allow your voice and a pause to add the impact of the quote to sink in. Make sure you are comfortable with the passage you choose and only use one or two quotes in a short toast or speech.

Once the bride and groom have entered the room and the guests are all seated, it is time for the best man's toast. If the reception is in a large room, make sure you have a microphone so that all guests can hear you. If there is a podium, by all means use it. It is perfectly acceptable to deliver your toast from notes or cue cards, and the podium will give you a place to rest your notes.

While you may be feeling nervous, it is most unlikely that anyone will notice. Therefore, there is no reason to announce to anyone that you are nervous. In fact, by doing so, you may be adding fuel to the fire. Your objective is to honor the bride and groom, not to talk about your nervousness.

Realize that you've often been in the company of nervous people without ever knowing it.

TIPS TO HELP RELAXATION

The thought of getting up in front of a sizeable crowd is turning your knees to jelly. Don't worry—there are several tricks that you can use to help yourself relax:

Try tensing and relaxing your jaw and neck muscles. Now do the same thing with the muscles of your stomach and upper torso.

Slowly breathe deeply in and out several times to the count of ten.

Press your thumb firmly into your left breastplate for a moment or two.

Sit quietly while envisioning yourself on a South Sea island.

In the unlikely event that you become totally unable to face up to the task, you can always apologize and back out. If that is unacceptable (and we certainly hope it is), a trip to a good hypnotist several days before the event can work wonders. Believe it or not, the hypnotist can program you to deliver your toast without any anxiety whatsoever. The fee could be very well worth it and the experience itself is worth having. The other option is to select one of our book's shortest toasts—some are as short as six words!

Whatever method of relaxation you use, nothing will work nearly as well as being fully prepared through practice, practice, practice.

THINGS TO AVOID

Let's talk now about some potential trouble spots that you'll want to stay away from. For instance, avoid making any negative statements about yourself and—really important—the bride or groom, or, for that matter, any members of the wedding party or family. Remarks such as, "I'm glad John finally found a job before he got married," or, "Isn't it wonderful that Mary managed to lose twenty pounds?" are inappropriate, to say the least. Neither should you begin your speech by anticipating your own failure, with remarks such as, "I'm not a good toastmaster and never have been, but I will try to do my best."

Avoid being overly solicitous or syrupy with excessive use of flowery language. Avoid statements such as, "I'm deeply and forever grateful for the opportunity to participate in this momentous occasion and consider this to be the highlight of my miserable, wormy existence." We have found that it is always best to speak in a natural, relaxed manner.

How To Do It

Okay, the time has come to deliver your toast.
Look squarely at the couple being toasted, then
move your gaze around to other people in the
room. Do not fix your gaze on the floor or wall.
Take a deep breath, be sure that the volume of your
voice is adequate to the occasion, and that everyone can hear you without straining. Try to speak
slowly and clearly, smile, relax, be real, and feel
the emotion of the moment. You'll be great!

Wedding Toasts

General Toasts

We have tried to include something for everyone in this section. Feel free to use these toasts as is, or combine several of them to make a longer toast. You may also want to include some lines of poetry or a Scripture verse.

Both Parents Toast

When children find true love, parents find true joy. Here's to your joy and ours from this day forward.

We wish you a beautiful wedding day and a fulfilling life together. May each new day bring you a new way to share your happiness with each other.

To John and Mary: We wish you both a long and happy life together. Knowing you are so happy makes us happy, because we love you so much.

Our wish for you both, is that you always remain a part of each other, even when apart.

May your married life hold the fulfillment of all your dearest dreams, and may your happiness be overflowing.

To John and Mary: It is our fondest wish that your life together will bring you closer and closer, and that you may fill your days with kisses, hugs and laughter.

We wish you a love that grows minute after minute, hour after hour, season after season, and year after year.

We all know that you two were made for one another. It shows in the way you relate to each other, and the way you look and listen to each other. From this day forward, may you nourish and cherish the love that you share.

The joys you are sharing today are overwhelming us with emotion. As your parents, it means the world to us to see you so happy. May your joy be complete and may you have a wonderful life together.

TOAST TO A DAUGHTER
It is with great pleasure that we welcome John into our family. It is obvious that Mary is happier today than we have ever seen her before. Having come to know John, we understand her joy. He is a happy,

confident, and stable man, who inspires confidence in all who know him. We are certain Mary has chosen a lifetime partner, and for that we rejoice. Each of them is happy on their own, neither relying on the other to "make them happy." Let us raise our glasses together to wish them all the best that life can bring.

As you've grown and matured, you have brought more joy and happiness to our lives than we ever believed possible. Now that you are entering this new phase of your life, we wish you the same pleasure that you have given to us, and a lifetime filled with blessings and happiness.

When you were born, we were overwhelmed with the love we felt for you. We've watched you grow and mature into the beautiful woman you are today. As you and John begin your life together, we wish you every blessing, and ask that you receive the same measure of happiness that you have brought to us.

TOAST TO A SON

We have watched you grow from boyhood to manhood, appreciating along the way, the very fine person you have become. We wish you and Mary a life filled with happiness, joy and success.

Having you as a son has been one of life's greatest gifts. Today, we begin to share our blessings with Mary. May the two of you know happiness beyond your wildest dreams.

You are a special couple brought together by the love that we have seen demonstrated in many ways. You fill each other with joy, and that makes us joyful too.

You have given us a wonderful gift—the gift of seeing our son and new daughter so much in love, and so committed to each other. May your love grow ever brighter, throughout each day of you lives together.

GENERAL TOASTS

On this very special day, it is my honor and pleasure to toast the sparkling couple you see before you. I am reminded, seeing John and Mary today, that love really knows no bounds, and occasionally manifests itself brilliantly in very special people. Let us stand and toast John and Mary: to a superb lifetime together.

It's a gift and a pleasure to share in your happiness today, and to wish for you both the best that life has to offer. May you achieve success to make you secure, trials to make you strong, luck to make life fun, and all of love's treasures to keep you happy.

To John and Mary: May your joys be as bright as the morning, and your sorrows but shadows that fade in the sunlight of love.

To John and Mary: You are two very special people who have the good fortune of having found each other. May you share exquisite happiness together all the days of your lives.

To John and Mary: May you always take time to laugh and dream, and to smell the flowers along your way.

To John and Mary: May you be blessed with courage, laughter, and hope, all the days of your lives.

To John and Mary: On this special day and forever more, may you be filled with happiness, and may all of your dreams come true.

To John and Mary: To your happiness, good health and cheer today, and every day for all your years.

To John and Mary: Here's to hours brightened by sunshine, days blessed by a happy marriage, and a lifetime filled with the love of friends and family.

Here's to love, here's to laughter.
Here's to great blessings forever after.
May love be always yours to give,
And may you share the joy of each moment
For as long as you both shall live.

To John and Mary: We wish you happiness that
deepens, love that grows stronger each day, and joy
and fulfilment in your new life together.

We wish you every happiness as you build your
lives and future together. Here's to the new husband, here's to the new wife. May they remain
lovers for all of their life.

To John and Mary: Nothing is as important as the
love you share. Take care of it, guard, protect and
nurture it every day of your lives.

Here's to a marriage built on trusting and caring,
and to the fulfillment of all the dreams you share.

To John and Mary: Remember the vows you've
taken on this joyous day, and may the love you
share sweep you along life's journeys with laughter
and grace.

To John and Mary: Remember to always take care
of the minutes, and the hours and days will take
care of themselves.

To John and Mary: May this special day be wonderful, and may you continue to do all the things
that mean the most to you.

To John and Mary: May your hopes become
realities, may your dreams become tomorrow's
memories, and may you always be happy together.

To John and Mary: May your lives be full of the things that are most important to you—love, laughter, children, and family. Here's to joy over-flowing.

The blending of two hearts is the best reason to celebrate. Let us raise our glasses to this beautiful couple—may they always be as happy as they are this moment.

We all have noticed the way John looks at Mary, and the way that Mary responds to John. May their love as a couple grow and deepen, strengthened by grace and joy.

The light surrounding this happy couple can be clearly seen by all. We are so delighted that you have found each other to share your dreams with. May your lives be long and happy.

To John and Mary: May your love be the base that

your lives are built on. May you grow closer and closer with each passing day.

To John and Mary: May your marriage be a pillar of strength, beauty, and love, and a shining example of two lives intertwined into one.

To John and Mary: May love be the rainbow and the light in both of your hearts and lives.

To John and Mary: May the vows and promises you made today be the mortar that binds you in your marriage. May your children be the expression of your love for each other, and may you have a long and happy life together.

To John and Mary: So often we get caught up in the daily busy-ness of everyday life that we forget to pay attention to the really important things. May you always make the time for each other, so that your relationship will grow and deepen, and become the most important thing in your lives.

To John and Mary: May you face life's joys and sorrows together, bound as one by the shimmering, silvery ribbon of love.

To John and Mary: May you always excite, delight and ignite each other!

To John and Mary: Down the hatch to a striking match.

May you always honor one another in a marriage filled with love. This truly is the best that life has to offer.

Let us raise our glasses to the happy couple: Here's to the groom with a bride so fair, and here's to the bride with a groom so rare.

May your life be filled with sun-baked beaches, hazy vineyards, and lazy lunches under Parisian umbrellas. May you always live your life in the moment, and may you enjoy a long, lingering, and always smoldering desire for each other.

To John and Mary: two terrific people. May the love you feel grow and flourish. May your home resonate with peace and harmony. May your family life be full, and may you have lots of beautiful, big, healthy babies.

To the happy couple: You showed great wisdom in choosing one another. May you spend your lives making right choices and remain forever in love.

To John and Mary: May your dreams come true, and may you always have something to wish for.

May your love grow and deepen in the years ahead, and may you be blessed with all the loves and joys of a happy marriage.

As the wedding bells ring out for you today, may you always have a home that's filled with laughter and happiness, joy and forgiveness.

On your wedding day and always, may love and blessings be yours in abundance.

As you remember the words that made you man and wife today, may you always consider each other in all things, place each other's needs ahead of your own, and may you value the unity that you share in love.

May all the love that's in your hearts grow deeper, year by year, and the memories of your wedding day remain forever dear.

To John and Mary: May this be the start of a bright, joyful, and fulfilling life together.

To John and Mary: A marriage built on trust and caring is what brings deepest meaning to life. Here's to the union of two hearts sharing one dream, one life, and one love, forever.

Here's to the bride and here's to the groom and here's to a happy honeymoon! May it last for all your days.

To John and Mary: May the most you wish for be the very least you receive.

May the fire of love that keeps you warm be always as hot as the weather is cold.

From this day forward, may you bring each other
all the happiness of life, and the beauty of love.

May your love grow more joyous and free from
care,
And may your life grow more beautiful with each
day you share.

To John and Mary: May you grow old together
sharing one pillow.

To John and Mary: May you forever be blessed
with the gifts of a happy marriage.

Here's to you both, a beautiful pair
On this, the beginning of your great love affair.

We wish you love that is ever caring, ever deepening, everlasting. Have a fabulous married life together.

Today your life together begins. May you be blessed with all the gifts of a happy marriage.

May your love multiply with the sharing of things that make you laugh and cry, and may your delight in each other brighten every day.

When two lives form one, a new sharing is begun. May you each grow to your own potential, and may you delight in the unity of the bond you share.

The greatest kind of love is one that is ever present, despite life's ups and downs. May your bond remain sure, and become deeper with each passing day.

To John and Mary: May your love be always
there, full of kindness, tolerance, and special
understanding.

May the love and friendship that you share grow
stronger with each breath you take.

On this special day, it's wise to pause and remi-
nisce about all you have shared so far, and to be
thankful for all that you have to look forward to.

The love you share is like the circle that forms
your ring. It is a symbol of the many joys your life
will bring.

As you begin your lives together and the years
unfold,
May the special joys of marriage by yours to have
and to hold.

To John and Mary: May your love for each other grow and deepen during your years together.

Love is the greatest miracle of all, because everything prospers and grows in its light and warmth.

Marriage, like life, has its ups and downs. When two people give and share love in great measure, the road ahead becomes easier and more beautiful to behold. May your love warm your journey, and may your hearts grow together.

To John and Mary: Two lives, two hearts, sharing one dream forever.

How fortunate you both are. You have found someone to be close to, someone you thought you would never find. You have someone to stand by you through happy and troubled times, someone to rejoice with, and share all the good that is to come. Let us raise our glasses to your union.

Today is the beginning of a beautiful forever. May your home be filled with joy, love, and laughter.

As the two of you repeat the vows that make you man and wife, may you be forever mindful that you are joined for life.

To John and Mary: May this be the beginning of the happiest days of your lives.

May all the love that's in your heart grow deeper every year, and may the memories of your wedding day remain forever dear.

To John and Mary: May your marriage continue to grow in love and friendship. May good fortune, honor, joy, and laughter always sustain you in your journey together.

To John and Mary: Let us toast to your two hearts together, loving and caring, giving and sharing, for the rest of your days.

May happiness and good fortune accompany John and Mary every day of their lives. May they always delight in each other.

To John and Mary: Let today be the beginning of a long and successful life, infused with love and understanding, through all the wonderful times to come. May the memory of this joyful day sustain you both through thick and thin, happy and sad.

All of us gathered here today are aware of the love and respect that exists between John and Mary. When they are together, they light up the darkest room. May they live their lives forever in this light.

John and Mary—one cannot think of one without the other. The joy of their union brings happiness to all of us who surround them.

As this day ends, it will mark the close of the first of many, many joyful days in the lives of John and Mary. May they be blessed with good fortune at every turn of their lives together.

To John and Mary: May they live every day of their lives in wedded bliss, knowing only prosperity and happiness, through even the most difficult of times.

To John and Mary: Together they are now one. May they live a long, happy, and prosperous life in this partnership. May their troubles be small, and their joys many.

To John and Mary: A new era has begun, an era of sharing strength and security with each other. May their lives be blessed with happiness, prosperity, and love.

To John and Mary: You are truly blessed as a couple. Not only do you share a great love for each other, you have the added blessing of being best friends. May the friendship and love you share, grow each day, for the rest of your lives.

Let's toast John and Mary: May their life together be filled with at least as much happiness as they are experiencing this very moment.

May John and Mary have a long, happy, and fruitful life together, filled with accomplishment, joy, and serenity.

May the sun always shine on this beautiful couple, and may all their hopes and dreams be fulfilled.

To John and Mary: May you spend the rest of your days loving and caring for each other, as much as you do today.

To John and Mary: We pray that success, happiness, and achievement be yours in all you do, and that your life together be filled with contentment.

Hail the Bridegroom—Hail the Bride!
Now the nuptial knot is tied.

We are delighted to be here, on this very special occasion, celebrating with John and Mary. May their love and affection grow with each passing day.

To John and Mary: A spark ignited a bonfire of passion and love between you. May the fires burn brightly for the rest of your days.

To John and Mary: May your eyes always see the beauty in each other. May those loving images continue to fuel the passion and love you share today.

To John and Mary: May you always know that your love for each other can conquer any problem you face, as long as you face it together.

To John and Mary: May the love you feel for each other deepen and grow stronger with each passing day. Here's to a lifetime of togetherness.

May your great love for one another always over- come your differences of opinion, for love surely conquers all.

To John and Mary: May your love continue to grow and may you always remain as happy as your are today.

To John and Mary: It is our wish that your lives be filled to overflowing with love and affection. May you respect each other, and may your nights together get you through whatever difficult days may come.

To John and Mary: May you live a full, happy, and creative life together, and may misfortune never touch you.

We rejoice in the union of John and Mary, and pray that their lives together give them each joy and happiness, beyond their greatest expectations.

May your lives be full and rewarding. May you savor the time you spend together, and may every hope and dream be realized.

To the newlyweds: May "for better or worse" be

far better than worse.

May you be ten times better off one year from now than you are today. May you never forget what is worth remembering, or remember what is best forgotten.

To John and Mary: Here's to you, a beautiful couple at the beginning of a life-long love affair.

To John and Mary: To your health and happiness, and may all your troubles be little ones.

To John and Mary: May this vow you've made today keep you happily engaged for the rest of your days.

To John and Mary: May the bread you break be more than bread, and may the music you hear be more than music. Here's to the happy couple.

Let the bells clang from every steeple,
While crying out to all the people.
John and Mary on his day have wed,
And on this eve will share a bed.
Here's to a long and exciting life together.

To John and Mary: May this journey of marriage
take you to warm, wonderful places, and may you
achieve things you never dreamed were possible.

May this path you are beginning today, lead you to
knowledge and light, wisdom and understanding,
tolerance and forgiveness. And may you grow old
together in the same bed.

To John and Mary: May you both live to be one
hundred, with one year extra to repent.

May laughter and happiness enrich every moment of your lives. May all your dreams come true, and bring you both untold happiness.

To John and Mary: May you spend your lives together knee deep in milk and honey.

We greet your new life with bells, streamers and confetti, music, dancing, and hearfelt wishes for a long and happy life together.

To John and Mary: Here's to you both—wherever you roam, may you always have a place you call home.

To John and Mary: Let love, honor, and respect be your constant companions, from this day forward.

To John and Mary: Here's to the light that lights

your eyes. May it continue to grow wondrously brighter for the rest of your days.

To John and Mary: Here's to the present, goodbye to the past. May you stay in love to the very last.

May your lives be filled with ease and grace, and may you always be thankful for one another.

May laughter, pure joy, and love for each other be with you all the days of your lives. May you never tire of being together, and may the future hold great happiness and contentment.

Here's to life's three greatest blessings: marriage, friends and children.

May all the pleasures of life be yours to share as husband and wife.

To John and Mary: May this special day be wonderful, and may the future bring all the things that mean the most to you.

To John and Mary: With each new day, may you always be discovering new ways to make each other happy.

Here's to a long and exciting life spent together, full of wonder, grace and love.

To John and Mary: May you always know, throughout the days your life together, that when one door closes, another will open.

To John and Mary: May your world together be as wonderful as the hopes you share this day, and may your life be filled with fine music and dancing.

To John and Mary: May you be poor in misfortune and rich in every blessing, all the days of your lives.

It is said that "into each life a little rain must fall." When the rain appears, may it be no stronger than a light mist.

To John and Mary: We wish you a lifetime woven with joyous laughter, and filled with passionate love.

To John and Mary: May you continue to celebrate your marriage forever, and may you always remain beautiful in each other's eyes.

May your wedding day be filled with great hopes and glorious dreams, and may you have a long and happy lifetime to make them all come true.

To John and Mary: You have received the great
gift of sharing your lives together. Do it joyfully,
for the rest of your days.

To John and Mary: May you find every happiness
life has to offer, and may you remain forever in
love with one another.

Here's to John and Mary: May the happiest day of
your past be the saddest day of your future.

To John and Mary, whose intellectual paths
brought them together as one. May they share a
full, prosperous, and successful life together.

To two very special people who found a very
special love. We wish you happiness and a wonderful life together.

When two people fall in love, it is a wonderful
thing to see their lives begin to blend into one. On
this important day, may you continue to walk in
harmony and love.

Every moment you spend together is special, but
none more so than this day. May you share a
lifetime of sublime happiness and deep compassion for each other, and may you value your bond
as husband and wife above all things. Let us all
raise our glasses and drink to the bride and groom.

To John and Mary: We wish you many years filled
with happiness and wonderful memories, all at
least as wonderful as today. May love and good
fortune come your way from every corner of the
earth.

To John and Mary: Love is the music of the heart
and marriage is the happiest song. May your lives
be always harmonious, filled with laughter and

grace, compassion and forgiveness.

To John and Mary: May the love that's in your hearts today grow and deepen. And may you always cherish, treasure, and believe in each other for as long you live.

To John and Mary: May every day of your marriage be another wedding day, and may you always share this strong commitment, with no reservations or conditions.

To John and Mary: After this wonderful celebration, and after the excitement of the honeymoon, you get to begin the greatest part—your life together as husband and wife.

We wish you all of the ingredients for a happy life—love, creative fulfillment, joy, and success.

To John and Mary: You have undergone trials and tribulations, and suffered reversals, yet you came through these to discover each other. How wonderful and how blessed you are!

May the rhythm of happiness and eternal joy beat loudly in your heart.

May you live forever in love, and may love live forever in you.

We wish you a special joy, now that your wedding day is here. May you share pride in all the accomplishments you two will achieve throughout your years together.

LOVE AT FIRST SIGHT
John met Lois, and he knew, at that instant, that he would spend the rest of his life with her. May this love that ignited at first sight, grow in intensity over the years of their lives together.

To John and Mary: May this whirlwind romance that has engulfed you, continue on for the rest of your lives.

John and Mary fell in love the moment they met. May they always stay in love—today, tomorrow, next year, next decade, and all through eternity.

When John met Mary, he was thunderstruck, bowled over by love at first sight. That feeling only grew and deepened as he got to know Mary, and their lives began to intertwine. May the passion of their love grow and change over the years to become the foundation of a large, happy, and boisterous family life, filled with soccer games, ballet lessons, birthday parties, and family celebrations.

FOR STAR GAZERS
Jupiter is known as the planet of "Great Beneficence," bringing good fortune, and the fusion of

the head and the heart. May Jupiter reign supreme in these areas of your lives together, and may you always love, honor, and respect each other.

The gods rejoiced when you finally met. They knew your destiny was to be together as soul mates for all eternity.

FOR SAILORS
To John and Mary: May the winds of good fortune carry you to wherever you want to be for all the days of your lives.

May you never lack sunny skies, warm breezes, and smooth sailing. May your horizons be clear, and may the wind be always at your back.

To John and Mary: May this ship of marriage have no mishaps. May it never founder or run aground, and may the gentle currents deliver you to paradise.

To John and Mary: May your life be full of excitement and tranquility, sunny skies and refreshing shade, smooth sailing and swift journeys. May you be lashed together through the storms that come, and through the peaceful days of golden sunshine.

To John and Mary: May your marriage be as graceful as a sailing sloop, gliding across tranquil waters.

SPIRITUAL
Love is a gift given by God, with no strings attached. May you treasure and guard it for the rest of your life.

To John and Mary: May God be your partner throughout your married life, and may He always guide you as husband and wife.

May the Lord love you, but not call you too soon.

To John and Mary: May God make your union a perfect example of what marriage was meant to be.

To John and Mary—a marriage made in heaven. May God bless and keep you safe, and may this union be tied together with the bonds of love.

Our wish for you, this very special day, is that God will greatly bless your marriage. May you, John, be a loving, faithful, and supportive husband, and may you, Mary, be a loving, faithful, and supportive wife. May you grow together and separately, and may your fondest wish come true.

To John and Mary: May you both enter heaven together—but late!

As you begin your life together, may you feel
God's presence to guide you, and may He always
keep you far from fear.

May your marriage be based on the goodness and
the mercy of God. May you seek His will in all
things, and may you never doubt His presence in
your lives.

To John and Mary: Your marriage was certainly in
the stars. We who know you, see the wisdom of
God shining through the two of you. We wish you
a completely fulfilling and happy life together.

John and Mary have offered to each other, God's
greatest gift—their lives. They have sure knowledge that they were meant to be together. May their
lives be blessed with joy and happiness.

To John and Mary: Our hope is that your lives will
always be illuminated by God's grace, and that the

number of your days be many.

May the angels and saints protect you, and may sorrow neglect you, all the days of your lives.

To John and Mary: We pray that what God has joined together this day, remain together, joyfully lived forever.

To John and Mary: Your love is a direct gift of a gracious God. May you always treasure it, guard and nurture it, throughout your days together.

To John and Mary: May you always be aware of the powerful forces in the heavens that brought you together. May you remain forever thankful, and may you delight in each other's presence every day of your lives.

John and Mary have been called into the bond of marriage by God. May their love burn as brightly as the sun, until the end of their days.

Today is the first day of the rest of your lives together. May your love be there to warm you when you're cold, soothe you when you're hurt, fill you when you're hungry, and sustain you when the going gets rough. May you always look to God to walk beside you, and keep you close to Him and to each other, through all your years together.

To John and Mary: May your days be filled with laughter and happiness, and may you keep in mind the prayer of St. Francis:

"O Master, grant that I may never seek
so much to be consoled as to console,
to be understood as to understand,
to be loved as to love with all my soul."

Here's to a long life and a happy love affair.

To John and Mary: We who know you, know your

deep spiritual commitment to God, and to each other. May the Lord bless your union, increase your faith, and bind you ever closer to one another. May you always walk hand in hand, in peace and love.

To John and Mary: May your love for each other grow day by day. May you be blessed with warmth, happiness, and contentment. And may you always, "seek first the kingdom of God," for it is only then that your lives will truly be fulfilled.

May you always think of yourselves as one person. May your lives be filled with love and compassion, and may the wisdom of the Lord surround you and direct you, all the days of your lives together. God bless you and keep you.

May the Lord God bless your marriage with His most precious gifts: love, joy, peace, goodness, and patience.

May your love grow like a tree planted by running water that yields abundant fruit, and has leaves that never fade.

WEDDING TOASTS

Toasting Each Other

This is a relatively new and, we think, charming custom. At some point after the toast from the best man, the groom toasts the bride in their new life together. The bride may respond by toasting her groom.

TOAST FROM THE GROOM TO THE BRIDE

Your smile and laughter brings God's love to everyone you meet. For certain, the world is a better place because of you. I am so proud to be your husband.

You make me so much happier than I thought I could ever be. I want the joy that we feel right now to last forever. Here's to you, my sweet.

Think of how much our lives have changed since we first met. I don't ever want to take you for granted. I don't ever want to forget how empty my life was before you came along. What a lucky man I am. Here's to our life together.

Here's to the love of my life, the light of my eyes, the darling of my heart. On this day of days, I honor you.

I know that years from now, we will look back on this day and it will seem so far away. This is our starting point, our beginning. The road ahead is uncertain, but together we will navigate the many twists and turns, firmly holding on to each other, always stopping to enjoy the view and to smell the roses. Here's to you!

The moment I saw you in your beautiful wedding dress, I thought my heart would burst with love and pride. Thank you for being my partner, my soulmate, my friend, my lover, my wife. Everyone please join me, raise your glasses and toast my beautiful bride.

I will try to give you all the wonderful things of life, but the one thing I can promise you is that I will love you for all the seasons of my life.

Because I love you, I want to walk with you for the rest of my life, hand in hand, through the years to come. Here's to our future together.

TOAST FROM THE BRIDE TO THE GROOM
I want our love and togetherness to continue to grow, beyond this moment, beyond tomorrow, and into eternity. Here's to my wonderful husband.

Before we met, the idea of a soulmate was incomprehensible to me. Then you came along, and I discovered in you a person who knows my every thought, feels my emotions, makes me laugh, and touches my heart. I discovered the comfort and peace which only comes from finding the companion of your heart, and I know, with certainty, that we were created for each other. Here's to life's beginnings.

To John: Our love is so powerful, so special. Here's to our life together and to the days of happiness ahead.

My handsome groom: My heart is so full right now, my eyes are filled with tears of happiness and joy. I am so grateful that we have found each other, and are starting off on our road of life. I know that this moment will shine brightly in our memories. I love you—you are my knight in shining armor, my friend, my love.

Wherever you are is where I want to be. Wherever you will travel, I will travel beside you, through all our adventures, happy and sad, for the rest of our days.

Until I fell in love with you, I never realized that any one person could fill my life so completely. You changed my life and made it dramatically better. I hope I have changed yours in the same way. Here's to our beginning.

To John: You brighten my world with your very warm and generous ways. You add the missing ingredient that I've been searching for all my life. When I'm counting my blessings, I always thank God for bringing us together.

I love you. I love everything about you—your smile, your beautiful voice, and that adventurous twinkle in your eyes. May we always see each other as we do this day.

You'll always have my love in your life. I will encourage and believe in you, because your every joy is my joy. This is my promise, my love, to you.

The Bride and Groom
Toast Their Families

S o many emotions crowd around us as we are preparing to get married. We are thrilled and excited at the prospect of this new commitment to our beloved, but, also, there is a touch of sadness as our relationship with our parents undergoes a shifting of focus.

We have put together a selection of toasts as the bride and groom honor their families. Pick and choose from among them to create your own heartfelt messages.

TOASTS TO THE PARENTS

I love you both so much. I feel blessed beyond all

telling, for you have shown me what it's like to be loved without reservation. You have always been there to watch over me and protect me, yet you have given me the freedom to grow and to find myself. Thank you for all the qualities you have shown me: love, strength, compassion, generosity, and fearlessness. I hope you will always be proud of me.

I am so thankful that you are my parents. You have shown me what life and love is all about. Your love for each other has given me an understanding of what it takes to have a successful marriage. Your love for me is always with me, as warm and cozy as my favorite blanket. Thank you for always being there, thank you for your love, thank you for everything.

Mom and Dad: You have taught me to expect the most from myself, and to always be ready to help someone else. Your spirit of love and compassion has been an inspiration to me all my life. On our wedding day, John and I honor you.

Mom and Dad: Your lifelong relationship has been an example to all who know you. On this happy day, I thank you for the gifts you have given to me—love, laughter, direction, expectations, and compassion. I hope that my life will honor yours.

Mom and Dad: Being raised as your daughter has taught me firsthand about love and what it takes to be a family. You allowed me just the right amount of freedom, so that I always felt cherished and valued as a person. Even when I was a teenager and I was so trying, you made me feel secure in your love. You always encouraged me to do my best, and to be myself. Thank you for everything.

I am so grateful for all of your loving care. You have always been there for me whenever I needed you, and John and I will always be there for you. We love you.

Thank you for the braces, the computer, ballet lessons, my bike, my brothers and sisters, and the million and one things that you have given me over the years. But most of all, I thank God that He gave me you as my parents. Cheers.

Our house was always full of fun, laughter, music, and people. You taught me so much about life, about not taking myself too seriously, and about how to always listen with an open heart. Thank you for being such wonderful parents.

I have certainly lived a privleged life under your roof. It seemed that nothing was too much to ask for. But the most important thing that you gave me was, and is, your love and affection, along with guidance and a firm purpose for my life. Thank you for being such strong, loving parents.

What wonderful parents you are! Your love for me has been unfailing, even though times have not always been so easy. One of the things you have taught me is that situations may change, but our love for each other is constant. Thank you for the wonderful home you provided for me. I love you more than I can say.

Mom and Dad: I have always had the feeling that you two were my real-life, in-the-flesh, guardian angels. You rescued me more times than I like to think about. Heaven only knows the situations that were prevented because of your loving intervention. Somehow, you saved me from all those terrible boy friends, unsuitable career choices, and other near catastrophes.

Well, Mom and Dad, you can now breathe a sigh of relief. Your good teaching has led me to John, the man I love with all my heart. Thank your for showing me the way.

You have taught me so very much. Our family has not always had it easy—we've had our share of heartbreaks. You have taught me, through your steadfast faith in God and in each other, that unexpected blessings can sometimes come out of apparently tragic events. You have shown me that, with love and laughter, life is, indeed, beautiful. I hope I can live my life with the strength, humor, compassion, and grace that you live yours. Thank you for giving me such valuable gifts.

Mom and Dad: Thank you for giving me the freedom to be myself. You allowed me to grow and flouish, and to become the slightly nutty, offbeat person you see today! Here's to you.

Thank you for always allowing me to express myself freely, even if you didn't always agree with me. You have always made me feel valuable as a person, and loved as a son. I love you.

Mom and Dad: You have taught me that our future is built on the choices that we make each day. Thank you for your insights, your love and devotion, and, most of all, your example.

You've taught me so much—how can I possibly express what you mean to me? You've taught me to appreciate the beauty that we see all around us, the magnificence of our natural world, and the order and wonder of our universe. Most of all, thank you for your unconditional love, unlimited patience, and gentle guidance.

Mom and Dad: I am so grateful for the strong, loving relationship we've always had, and I'm so happy that you consider Mary to be your new daughter. Here's to our future life together, and the many new facets it will bring to all of us.

I've learned how to live by your example, and by this simple prayer that you've taught me: "God grant me the serenity to accept the things I cannot change, the courage to change the things I can, and the wisdom to know the difference." May we all always have that wisdom.

Thank you for all that you've done for me my whole life long. You've always encouraged me to do the very best I can, and then to leave the outcome to God. I am so grateful that you're my parents and I love you both very much.

Mom and Dad: You've shown me that life can be lived with enthusiasm, vitality, freedom, and a feeling of well being, if we have a solid connection to God. Thank you for sharing your wisdom with me, and I hope that I can live my life in the same joyful way that you have lived yours.

Mom and Dad: You two are hopeless romantics, and I have been privileged to be part of your great love affair. Thank you for setting such a wonderful example.

You are both great teachers. By your example, you've shown me how to persevere in a marriage, and how to be honest with myself and my partner. I hope I may always make you proud.

Mom and Dad: I have never once doubted your love for me. You have always given me a warm, devoted, secure feeling as I was growing up. I know now that this is your special gift to me, and I thank you with all my heart.

Mom and Dad: I can honestly say that our life as a family has never once been boring! Through all the ups and downs we've experienced together, there was always one constant—our strong love for each other. Thank you for the exciting ride, the laughter, the fun, and, most of all, your consuming love for me. I love you both.

All of my important life lessons have been learned through the many changes we've experienced as a family. We've shared happiness and sadness, thrills and disappointments, and you've held on to your compassion and your sense of humor through it all. Thank you for giving me such a wonderful example on how to live life gracefully.

Thanks to your help and encouragement, I've been able to achieve my hopes and aspirations. You have always been a source of inspiration, love, and wisdom to me, and I love you both so much.

You have always shown me how to count my blessings and be grateful for all that I have been given. You've taught me, by your own example, how important it is to see the glass as "half full," instead of "half empty." Thank you for all you've done, for all the love you've given me, and for your loving presence in my life.

Mom and Dad: You've set my feet firmly on the road of faith and spirituality, which comforts me every hour of my life. Thank you for always sharing your wisdom with us.

Living with you two wonderful people all of my life has taught me the value of team work in a marriage. Thank you for your shining example.

Toasts to Siblings

Here's to my wonderful sister. We have had so much fun over the years—lots of fights, lots of laughs, lots of secrets. I'm so happy you're here to share this most special day with me. I love you and I want to thank you for being the best sister in the whole, wide world.

To my beautiful big sister: There are so many things I admire about you. I have watched you, copied you, and looked up to you, during our growing-up years, and learned a lot of life's most valuable lessons from our relationship. Thank you for being such a wonderful sister. I'm so grateful for your love and example.

The one thing I have never outgrown, and probably never will, is our close relationship and binding love. You have always been my greatest friend, my most ardent defender, and the best brother anyone could ever have.

To my brothers and sisters: No matter where life takes us, we will always have the special bond that only exists between brothers and sisters. We share the same memories, remember the same family vacations and holiday dinners. Growing up, we got into trouble together, knew each other's friends and failings, rejoiced at one another's successes, and, of course, drove poor Mom and Dad half crazy when we messed up. But most of all, we share the, sometimes unspoken, love and concern for each other. May we always be close.

To my sister: Thank you for letting me borrow your clothes, listen to your CDs, and use your make up. Thanks, too, for sticking up for me at school, helping me with my homework, and being the greatest secret keeper of all time! Here's to you.

To my big brother: You have always been the one to watch over me and keep me on the straight and narrow. I hope you know how much I love you and look up to you.

To my sister: When I think of our growing up years, I remember, most of all, the summer vacations, and the fun we had with each other. It seemed like all we did was giggle, swim, color, and fight. I can't believe that it was so long ago, and now here we are, all grown up at my wedding. Here's to a lifetime of giggling, sharing, and loving each other.

To my sister: Our memories are bound together as one. No matter what happens in our lives, we will always have that special closeness that only grows between sisters. I love you and thank you for being so terrific.

WEDDING TOASTS

Key Phrases for Your
Personalized Toast

We have gathered key phrases that will help you write your own personalized toast to the bride and groom. Select a phrase from each section, then add some lines that you particularly like from "General Toasts," or a verse or two of poetry from our "Great Poets and Sages" sections. It's always nice to include a short story or two about how the bride and groom met, or a funny incident that happened during their courtship. Make sure you have a beginning, a middle, and an end, and *Voila,* a toast is born!

BEGINNING

I am (happy/honored/thrilled/fortunate/blessed)at having been (chosen/asked) to speak on this most (wonderful/important/joyful) occasion.

I have known the (bride/groom) since (she/he) was a (child/teenager/college student). As a (brother/sister/cousin/aunt/uncle/friend/roommate/neighbor) I am honored to offer this toast.

MIDDLE

I have seen (Mary/John) grow into a (successful/well-rounded/happy/outgoing) person, full of (wisdom/generosity/beauty/grace).

(He/she) has spent a lot of time and effort developing (his/her) talents in (the arts/music/sports/intellectual pursuits).

(His/her/their) career as a (journalist/auto mechanic/lawyer/stock broker/artist/banker/actor) has shown their dedication and ability, and is sure to make their union (happy/stable/successful/interesting).

I have seen them grow from (friends/classmates/

co-workers/enemies) to lovers.

John and Mary both come from happy and stable
families, where they have learned the true meaning
of commitment.

Their (interests/careers) are (compatible with/
different from) each other and they come from
(similar/diverse) backgrounds.

ENDING

May they live (happily ever after/long and successful lives/together through all eternity/as husband
and wife forever/in peace and serenity/in love and
harmony/with joy in their hearts).

We wish you our very best of what life has to offer
for the rest of your days.

Let us raise our glasses and toast the happy couple.

Here's to you both.

Skoal!

WEDDING TOASTS

The Bible on Love and Marriage

For thousands of years, the Bible has guided us through the days of our lives. Here are just a few of the passages, from the Old and New Testaments, that we thought might be appropriate for this special day.

May your thoughts be wholly directed to all that is true, all that deserves respect, all that is honest, pure, admirable, decent, virtuous, or worthy of praise. Live according to what you have learned and accepted, what you have heard me say and seen me do. Then will the God of peace be with you.

Philipians 4:8-9

The Lord bless you and keep you! The Lord make his face to shine upon you, and be gracious to you: The Lord lift up his countenance upon you, and give you peace!

Numbers 6:24-26

That is why a man leaves his father and mother and clings to his wife; and the two of them become one body.

Genesis 2:24

Except the Lord build the house, they labor in vain that build it.

Psalm 127:1

Beloved, let us love one another: for love is of God.

1 John 4:7

If God is for us who can be against us?

Romans 8:31

As for me and my household we will serve the Lord.

Joshua 24:15

Forsaking all others, keep thee only unto her, so long as ye both shall live.

The Book of Common Prayer

If a house be divided against itself, that house cannot stand.

Mark 3:25

I have set before you life and death, the blessing and the curse. Choose life, then, that you and your descendents may live, by loving the Lord, your God, heeding his voice, and holding fast to him.

Deuteronomy 30:19-20

ON LOVE

Love is patient; love is kind, love is not jealous, it does not put on airs, it is not snobbish. Love is never rude, it is never self-seeking, it is not prone to anger; neither does it brood over injuries. Love does not rejoice in what is wrong but rejoices with the truth. There is no limit in love's forbearance, to its trust, to its power to endure.

Love never fails. Prophecies will cease, tongues will be silent, knowledge will pass away. When I was a child I used to talk like a child, think like a child, reason like a child. When I became a man I put childish ways aside. Now we see indistinctly, as in a mirror; then we shall see face to face. My knowledge is imperfect now; then I shall know. There are in the end three things that last: faith, hope and love, and the greatest of these is love.

1 Corinthians 13:4-8

Can two walk together, unless they have agreed?

Amos 3:3

God's love has been poured into our hearts through

the Holy Spirit which has been given to us.

Romans 5:5

It is not good that man should be alone. I will
make a suitable partner for him.

Genesis 2:18

Little children let us love in deed and in truth and
not merely talk about it.

1John 3:18

As the Father has loved me, so I have loved you.
Live on in my love.

John 15:9

We, for our part, love because he first loved us.

1John 4:19

The way we came to understand love was that he laid down his life for us.

1John 3:16

Love has no room for fear; rather, perfect love casts out all fear.

1John 4:18

The command that I give you is this, that you love one another.

John 15:17

Above all, let your love for each other be constant, for love covers a multitude of sins.

1Peter 4:8

God is love, and he who abides in love abides in God and God in him.

1John 4:16

This, remember, is the message you heard from the
beginning: we should love one another.

1John 3:10

Beloved, let us love one another because love is of
God; everyone who loves is begotten of God and
has knowledge of God. The man without love has
known nothing of God, for God is love.

1John 4:7-8

Beloved, if God has loved us, so we must have the
same love for one another.

1John 4:11

No one has ever seen God. Yet if we love one
another God dwells in us, and his love is brought
to perfection in us.

1John 4:12

How beautiful you are, how pleasing, my love, my
delight!

Song of Solomon 7:7

Let him kiss me with kisses of his mouth! More delightful is your love than wine!

Song of Solomon 1:2

As a lily among thorns, so is my beloved among women.

Song of Solomon 2:2

Strengthen me with raisin cakes, refresh me with apples, for I am faint with love.

Song of Solomon 2:5

My beloved speaks and says to me: Arise, my love, my fair one, and come away; for lo, the winter is past, the rain is over and gone. The flowers appear on the earth, the time of singing has come, and the voice of the turtledove is heard in our land.

Song of Solomon 2:8-12

Let us go early to the vineyards, and see if the vines are in bloom, if the buds have opened, if the pomegranates have blossomed; there will I give you my love.

Song of Solomon 7:11-13

Set me as a seal in your heart, as a seal on your arm; for stern as death is love, relentless as the nether world is devotion; its flames are a blazing fire. Deep waters cannot quench love, nor floods sweep it away. Were one to offer all he owns to purchase love, he would be roundly mocked.

Song of Solomon 8:6-7

ON HUSBANDS AND WIVES

And Ruth said: "Entreat me not to leave thee, or to return from following after thee: For wherever you go, I will go, and wherever you lodge, I will lodge. Your people shall be my people, and your God my God. Where you die, I will die, and there will I be buried beside you."

Ruth 1:16-17

I will espouse you to me forever: I will espouse
you in right and in justice, in love and in mercy; I
will espouse you in fidelity, and you shall know the
Lord.

Hosea 2:21-22

Husbands should love their wives as they do their
own bodies. He who loves his wife loves himself.
Observe that no one ever hates his own flesh; no,
he nourishes it and takes care of it as Christ cares
for the church, for we are members of his body.
For this reason a man shall leave his father and
mother, and shall cling to his wife, and the two
shall be made into one.

Ephesians 5:28-31

ON MARRIAGE

Two are better than one; they get a good wage for
their labor. If the one falls, the other will lift up his
companion. Woe to the solitary man! For if he
should fall, he has no one to lift him up. So also if
two sleep together, they keep each other warm.
How can one alone keep warm? Where a lone man
may be overcome, two together can resist. A three-
ply cord is not easily broken.

Ecclesiastes 4:9-12

Have you not heard that at the beginning the Creator made them male and female and declared, for this reason a man shall leave his father and mother and cling to his wife, and the two shall become as one? Thus they are no longer two but one flesh. Therefore, let no man separate what God has joined.

Matthew 19:4-6

ON HOME AND FAMILY

None of those who cry out, Lord, Lord, will enter the kingdom of God but only the one who does the will of my father in heaven.

Anyone who hears my words and puts them into practice is like the wise man who built his house on rock. When the rainy season set in, the torrents came and the winds blew and buffeted his house. It did not collapse; it had been solidly set on rock.

Anyone who hears my words but does not put them into practice is like the foolish man who built his house on sandy ground. The rains fell, the torrents came, the wind blew and lashed against his house. It collapsed under all this and was completely ruined.

Matthew 7:21, 24-27

Unless the Lord build the house, they labor in vain
who build it. Unless the Lord guard the city, in
vain does the guard keep vigil. It is vain for you to
rise early, or put off your rest. You that eat hard-
earned bread, for he gives to his beloved in sleep.

Psalm 127:1-2

Great Poets and Sages

Where would the poets be without the topic of love? Try to imagine a poet without love, or love without the beautiful language of the poets! Why not use one or more passages from these time-honored selections to add beauty and elegance to your toast.

How Do I Love Thee?
(from Sonnets from the Portugese*)*

How do I love thee?Let me count the ways.
I love thee to the depth and breadth and height
My soul can reach, when feeling out of sight

For the ends of Being and ideal Grace.
I love thee to the level of every day's
Most quiet need, by sun and candlelight.
I love thee freely, as men strive for Right;
I love thee purely, as they turn from Praise.
I love thee with the passion put to use
In my old griefs, and with my childhood's faith.
I love thee with a love I seemed to lose
With my lost saints—I love thee with the breath,
Smiles, tears, of all my life!—and, if God choose,
I shall but love thee better after death.

ELIZABETH BARRETT BROWNING

Shall I Compare Thee To A Summer's Day?
(Sonnet XVIII)

Shall I compare thee to a Summer's day?
Thou art more lovely and more temperate:
Rough winds do shake the darling buds of May,
And Summer's lease hath all too short a date:
Sometime too hot the eye of heaven shines,
And often is his gold complexion dimmed;
And every fair from fair sometime declines,
By chance or nature's changing course untrimmed:
But thy eternal Summer shall not fade
Nor lose possession of that fair thou owest;
Nor shall Death brag thou wanderest in his shade,
When in eternal lines to time thou growest:
So long as men can breathe, or eyes can see,
So long lives this, and this gives life to thee.

WILLIAM SHAKESPEARE

Married Love

You and I
Have so much love,
That it
Burns like a fire,
In which we bake a lump of clay
Molded into a figure of you
And a figure of me.
Then we take both of them,
And break them into pieces,
And mix the pieces with water,
And mold again a figure of you
And a figure of me.
I am in your clay,
You are in my clay.
In life we share a single quilt,
In death we share one coffin.

KUAN TAL SHENG,
13TH CENTURY A.D.

Grow old with me
The best is yet to be.
The last day of life, for which
The first is made.

ROBERT BROWNING

Look down you gods,
and on this couple drop a blessed crown.

WILLIAM SHAKESPEARE

It was not in the winter our love was cast!
It was the time of roses,
We plucked them as we passed!

THOMAS HOOD

Marriage: a community consisting of a master and
a mistress and two slaves, making in all, two.

AMBROSE BIERCE

To Celia
(from The Forest)

Drink to me only with thine eyes,
And I will pledge with mine;
Or leave a kiss but in the cup
And I'll not look for wine.
The thirst that from the soul doth rise
Doth ask a drink divine;
But might I of Jove's nectar sup,
I would not change for thine.

I sent thee late a rosy wreath,

Not so much honoring thee
As giving it a hope that there
It could not withered be;
But thou thereon didst only breathe,
And sent'st it back to me;
Since when it grows, and smells, I swear,
Not of itself but thee!

BEN JONSON

A Red, Red Rose

O, my luve's like a red, red rose
That's newly sprung in June;
O, my luve's like the melodie
That's sweetly played in tune.

As fair thou art, my bonnie lass,
So deep in luve am I;
And I will luve thee still my dear,
Till a' the seas gang dry.

Till a' the seas gang dry, my dear,
And the rocks melt wi' the sun;
I will luve thee still, my dear,
While the sands o' life shall run.

And fare-thee-weel, my only luve!
And fare-thee-weel a while!
And I will come again, my luve,
Though it were ten thousand mile.

ROBERT BURNS

The Passionate Shepherd to His Love

Come live with me and be my Love,
And we will all the pleasures prove
That hills and valleys, dales and fields,
Or woods or steepy mountain yields.

And we will sit upon the rocks,
And see the shepherds feed their flocks
By shallow rivers, to whose falls
Melodious birds sing madrigals.

And I will make thee beds of roses
And a thousand fragrant posies;
A cap of flowers, and a kirtle
Embroidered all with leaves of myrtle.

A gown made of the finest wool
Which from our pretty lambs we pull;
Fair-lined slippers for the cold
With buckles of the purest gold.

A belt of straw and ivy-buds
With coral clasps and amber studs;
And if these pleasures may thee move,
Come live with me and be my Love.

The shepherd swains shall dance and sing
For thy delight each May morning:
If these delights thy mind may move,

Then live with me and be my Love.

CHRISTOPHER MARLOWE

First Love

I ne'er was struck before that hour
With love so sudden and so sweet,
Her face it bloomed like a sweet flower
And stole my heart away complete.
My face turned pale a deadly pale.
My legs refused to walk away,
And when she looked, what could I ail?
My life and all seemed turned to clay.

And then my blood rushed to my face
And took my eyesight quite away,
The trees and bushes round the place
Seemed midnight at noon day.
I could not see a single thing,
Words from my eyes did start
They spoke as chords do from the string,
And blood burnt round my heart.

Are flowers the winter's choice?
Is love's bed always snow?
She seemed to hear my silent voice,
Not loves appeals to know.
I never saw so sweet a face
As that I stood before.
My heart has left its dwelling-place

And can return no more.

JOHN CLARE

Thomas a Kempis, in his, The Imitation of Christ, *writes of the ideal love of the devout person for God. These beautiful words, based on Book III, Chapter V, also apply to the wondrous love between a man and a woman.*

Love is a great thing, and good in every way. It alone makes heavy burdens light, and bears happy and sad things equally. It endures hardships with ease, and makes bitter things taste flavorful and sweet.

Nothing is sweeter than love, nothing higher, nothing stronger, nothing larger, nothing more joyful, nothing fuller, and nothing better in heaven or on earth.

Love knows no measure, but is endlessly fervent. It fears no burden or labor, complains of no impossibility, but believes all things are possible. Love is swift, pure, meek, joyous and glad, strong, patient, faithful, wise, and forbearing.

Love is steadfast, and, even when life becomes difficult, love perseveres, for without some sorrow or pain, we cannot live in love.

THOMAS A KEMPIS
Adapted by Lois Frevert

If Thou Must Love Me
(From "Sonnets from the Portugese")
XIV

If thou must love me, let it be for naught
Except for love's sake only. Do not say,
"I love her for her smile—her look—her way
Of speaking gently,—for a trick of thought
That falls in well with mine, and certes brought
A sense of pleasant ease on such a day"—
For these things in themselves, Beloved, may
Be changed, or change for thee,—and love, so
            wrought,
May be unwrought so. Neither love me for
Thine own dear pity's wiping my cheeks dry,—
A creature might forget to weep, who bore
Thy comfort long, and lose thy love thereby!
But love me for love's sake, that evermore
Thou mayst love on, through love's eternity.

ELIZABETH BARRETT BROWNING

True Love

True love is but a humble, low-born thing,
And hath its food served up in earthenware;
It is a thing to walk with, hand in hand,
Through the everydayness of this work-day world,
Baring its tender feet to every roughness,

Yet letting not one heart-beat go astray
From beauty's law of plainness and content—
A simple, fireside thing, whose quiet smile
Can warm earth's poorest hovel to a home

JAMES RUSSELL LOWELL

For Thy Sweet Love
Sonnet 29

When in disgrace with fortune and men's eyes
I all alone beweep my outcast state,
And trouble deaf heaven with my bootless cries,
And look upon myself and curse my fate,
Wishing me like to one more rich in hope,
Featured like him, like him with friends possessed,
Desiring this man's art, and that man's scope,
With what I most enjoy contented least;
Yet in these thoughts myself almost despising,
Haply I think on thee—and then my state,
Like to the lark at break of day arising
From sullen earth, sings hymns at heaven's gate;
For thy sweet love remembered, such weallth
brings
That then I scorn to change my state with kings.

WILLIAM SHAKESPEARE

Love

I love you,

Not only for what you are,
But for what I am
when I am with you.

I love you,
Not only for what
You have made of yourself,
But for what
You are making of me.

I love you
For the part of me
That you bring out;
I love you
For putting your hand
Into my heaped-up heart
And passing over
All the foolish, weak things
That you can't help
Dimly seeing there,
And for drawing out
Into the light
All the beautiful belongings
That no one else had looked
Quite far enough to find.

I love you because you
Are helping me to make
Of the lumber of my life
Not a tavern
But a temple;
Out of the works
Of my every day

Not a reproach
But a song. . .

AUTHOR UNKNOWN

O God of Love, To Thee We Bow

O God of Love, to Thee we bow,
And pray for these before Thee now,
That closely knit in holy vow,
They may in Thee be one.

When days are filled with pure delight,
When paths are plain and skies are bright,
Walking by faith and not by sight,
May they in Thee be one.

When stormy winds fulfill Thy will,
And all their good seems turned to ill,
Then, trusting Thee completely still,
May they in Thee be one.

What e'er in life shall be their share
Of quickening joy or burdening care,
In power to do and grace to bear,
May they in Thee be one.

Eternal Love, with them abide;
In Thee forever may they hide,
For even death cannot divide
Those whom Thou makest one.

WILLIAM VAUGHAN JENKINS

Marriage

Going my way of old,
Contented more or less,
I dreamt not life could hold
Such happiness.

I dreamt not that love's way
Could keep the golden height
Day after happy day,
Night after night.

WILFRED WILSON GIBSON

What God Hath Promised

God hath not promised
Skies always blue,
Flower-strewn pathways
All our lives through;
God hath not promised
Sun without rain,
Joy without sorrow,
Peace without pain.

But God hath promised
Strength for the day,
Rest for the labor,
Light for the way,

Grace for the trials,
Help from above,
Unfailing sympathy,
Undying love.

ANNIE JOHNSON FLINT

True Love
Sonnet 116

Let me not to the marriage of true minds
Admit impediments. Love is not love
Which alters when it alteration finds,
Or bends with the remover to remove.
O, no! it is an ever-fixed mark,
That looks on tempests and is never shaken;
It is the star to every wandering bark,
Whose worth's unknown, although his height be
taken.
Love's not Time's fool, though rosy lips and
cheeks
Within his bending sickle's compass come;
Love alters not with his brief hours and weeks,
But bears it out even to the edge of doom.
If this be error and upon me proved,
I never writ, nor no man ever loved.

WILLIAM SHEAKESPEARE

Who Does What in the Wedding Party

This chapter is devoted to outlining the traditional, non-toasting responsibilities assumed by members of the wedding party. Basically the wedding party is expected to be helpful to the bride and groom, and to do their part in making sure the big day goes without a hitch!

THE MAID OF HONOR

The maid of honor has many responsibilities, including paying for her wedding outfit and travel expenses. Other duties are as follows:

To help the bride choose her wedding dress

To help the bride address the wedding invitations

To plan the bridal shower for the bride, with the help of the bridesmaids

To keep the bride on schedule for various events

To help the bride get ready for the ceremony

To arrange the bride's train and veil before going up the aisle

To hold the bride's bouquet during the ceremony

To straighten the bride's train before the recessional

In addition, the maid of honor dances with the best man at the reception. The maid of honor, in general, is there to assist the bride with whatever needs she may have during her special day.

THE BEST MAN
The best man is financially responsible for expenses relating to his own travel and tuxedo rentals. He is also responsible for paying all the service personnel and the church fee for services

rendered the day of the wedding. In addition, the best man is the keeper of the rings during the wedding ceremony and, of course, he is the chief executive officer in charge of toasting the bride and groom at the reception. Other duties include:

Arranging the bachelor party for the groom

Keeping the groom on schedule

Delivering the groom to the wedding site

Waiting with the groom before the ceremony, and as the rest of the wedding party comes down the aisle

Escorting the maid of honor and dancing with her at the reception

Making the first wedding toast

Getting the bride and groom to the airport or train station

Returning all tuxedos to the rental company.

THE BRIDESMAIDS
The bridesmaids are required to pay the costs of

their wedding attire and travel expenses. They are required to participate in many of the pre-wedding day happenings and they, too, have a variety of responsibilities for the wedding. They are as follows:

To assist the maid of honor in planning the bridal shower

To attend all pre-wedding functions and rehearsals

To assist the bride before, during and after the ceremony.

THE USHERS
The ushers are responsible for their wedding attire and travel expenses. The ushers don't have many pre-wedding responsibilities—their work comes the day of the wedding. The ushers responsibilities are as follows:

To help the best man arrrange the bachelor party

To arrive one hour before the ceremony for photographs

To seat the bride's family on the left and the

groom's family on the right
To escort guests down the aisle:
   when the guest is female, offer your right arm
   when the guest is male, walk on his left side
   when a couple arrives, offer the female your
   right arm, and the male can follow behind.

After the mothers of the bride and groom are
seated, roll down the carpet, if applicable

Direct guests to the reception area from the
church

Sit at the head table next to the bridesmaids

Dance with the bridesmaids and other guests at
the reception.

WEDDING TOASTS

The Most Important Duty of All

As friends of the happy couple, all wedding attendants, family members, and guests, will wish the bride and groom the very best of happiness, good fortune, love, and success. Remember them in your prayers and support them in their union.

The wedding ceremony is just one day—their life together following the ceremony is what's truly important, for they are beginning their own family unit. Not one of us knows what lies ahead—instead we must put our faith and trust in God and in each other, and hold fast to one another in all things.

Toast Notes

_____

_____

_____

_____

_____

_____

_____

_____

_____

_____

_____

_____

_____

_____

_____

_____

_____

_____

_____

_____

_____

_____

_____

_____

Toast Notes

_____

_____

_____

_____

_____

_____

_____

_____

_____

_____

_____

_____

_____

_____

_____

_____

_____

_____

_____

_____

_____

_____

_____

Toast Notes

Toast Notes

Toast Notes

Toast Notes

Toast Notes